My First Team

CHEERLEADING

by BERNARD CONAGHAN

TABLE OF CONTENTS

Sight Words.......................................2
Words to Know.......................................3
Index.......................................16

A Pelican Book
SEAHORSE PUBLISHING

Teaching Tips for Caregivers and Teachers:

Research shows that one of the best ways for students to learn a new topic is to read about it.

Before Reading

- Read the title and predict what the book will be about.
- Read the "Words to Know" and discuss the meaning of each word.
- Read the back cover to see what the book is about.

During Reading

- When a student gets to a word that is unknown, ask them to look at the rest of the sentence to find clues to help with the meaning of the unknown word.
- Motivate students with praise and encouragement.

After Reading

- Discuss the main idea of the book.
- Ask students to give one detail that they learned in the book.

SIGHT WORDS

a	get	together
are	in	use
do	the	we

WORDS TO KNOW

cheerleading

pom-
poms

ready position

squad

tumbling

We do **cheerleading**.

cheerleading

We get in the **ready position.**

ready position

SB CHEER
SB CHEER
SB CHEER

We cheer together.

We use **pom-poms.**

pom-poms

We do **tumbling**.

tumbling

We are a cheerleading **squad**!

squad
MGC
MAGNETIC
CHEERLEADING

Index

cheer 9
pom-poms 10, 11
ready position 6, 7
squad 14, 15
tumbling 12, 13

Written by: Bernard Conaghan
Series Development: James Earley

Photos: Shutterstock

Library of Congress PCN Data
Cheerleading / Bernard Conaghan
My First Team
ISBN 979-8-8945-9251-0 (hard cover)
ISBN 979-8-8945-9265-7 (paperback)
ISBN 979-8-8945-9293-0 (EPUB)
ISBN 979-8-8945-9279-4 (eBook)
ISBN 979-8-8945-9307-4 (audio)
ISBN 979-8-8945-9321-0 (Read-Along)
Library of Congress Control Number:
2024946247

Printed in Canada/012025/CP20250101

Seahorse Publishing Company
www.seahorsepub.com

Published in the United States
Seahorse Publishing
PO Box 771325
Coral Springs, FL 33077

SEAHORSE PUBLISHING